How to Raise Budgies

A Newbie's Guide to Raising Australian Parakeets – for Profit and Pleasure

Dueep Jyot Singh

How to Series

Mendon Cottage Books

JD-Biz Publishing

All Rights Reserved.

No part of this publication may be reproduced in any form or by any means, including scanning, photocopying, or otherwise without prior written permission from JD-Biz Corp Copyright © 2016

All Images Licensed by Fotolia, Pixabay, and 123RF.

Disclaimer

The information is this book is provided for informational purposes only. The information is believed to be accurate as presented based on research by the author.

The author or publisher is not responsible for the use or safety of any procedure or treatment mentioned in this book. The author or publisher is not responsible for errors or omissions that may exist.

Our books are available at

1. Amazon.com
2. Barnes and Noble
3. Itunes
4. Kobo
5. Smashwords
6. Google Play Books

Download Free Books!

http://MendonCottageBooks.com

Table of Contents

Introduction 4
   Your Budgie as a Pet 5
Getting to Know More about Your Lovebird 11
Breeding Season 13
   Male or female budgie? 14
Different Colors of Budgies 17
   Choosing the Perfect Budgie Specimen 21
Housing for Your Birdies 24
   Advantages of Making Your Own Cages 25
   Tier boxes 28
   Drinking water fount 31
Diet for your birds 33
Management of Your Birds 36
Baby Chicks 39
Marketing your birds 45
Diseases and Treatment 48
Conclusion 51
Author Bio 53
Publisher 64

Introduction

Budgerigars, also known as the Australian parakeets, budgies, or lovebirds have begun to grow more popular as the best choice for a caged bird pet for children and also a bird for breeding and profit.

This book is now going to tell you all about how you can raise budgerigars, whether it is to bring cheer into your house, or just for breeding purposes.

Every year, more and more people are looking for the best pet choice for a pet perhaps to keep a little child amused and happy, and also to breed this undoubtedly very sweet and fascinating little bird.

Budgerigar societies are coming up all over the World, where the care, the breeding, and tips and techniques on how you can keep your little lovebirds happy and healthy are shared openly to other budgerigar breeders all over the World.

So before I tell you more about how you can indulge in either what is going to be a very amusing hobby, or perhaps give you a lifetime source of profit. The only problem is that once you keep them as pets, you may just not want to sell them!

Your Budgie as a Pet

My aunt has 30 pairs of these lovebirds, kept in her garden. And no way has she sold the babies. She just gives them away to relatives and responsible friends! Another friend wanted just one little bird, which even though is song- less, is still chirpy, merry, and just like a canary, brings happiness into any sort of gloomy atmosphere or room.

But auntie told her that no little bird deserved this sort of loneliness. The friend could not believe it. So remember that lovebirds are social little birds, and definitely cannot be happy alone. And she intended to leave that little bird all alone, in her house, and spend her time at the office, only to welcome her back when she came home tired.

Aunty told her that that little bird would soon fade away through loneliness and heartbreak, because it had nobody with which to talk, if she was away all day. But she said that she would do the talking, when she came home.

And she was asked how would she like it, talking in Spanish to a person who understands only Swahili? When she was talking about the price of silk stockings, the person with whom she was communicating was talking about the weather, and how bad it was for the flowers in her garden.

So unless one was a total motor mouth, capable of talking without rhyme or reason and without bothering whether somebody heard the talk or not, at least her little bird would have a little friend of its own, to which it could talk, communicate, gossip with, and keep itself occupied, all the time you were not around, because it is a total motor mouth.

It knows that you are around to give it food and water, and also to clean its cage, as well as to talk to it occasionally in some obscure vague sort of language. But it would rather have someone else of its own kind to which to chatter and complain!

And as it does not belong to your species, it is not going to trouble itself to come and talk to you, like real pet parrots do, or even dogs, unless of course it is a male bird. It is basically a wild bird, caged, but if the child raises it from a baby, as a pet, you can have it riding on a shoulder talking away, 19 to the dozen, into your ear. And it needs the occasional acknowledgment of something spoken by you, even though it is not listening! And so both of you can be happy in each other's company!

My parents kept three pairs, before they had any children to occupy them, and when dad went to the office, mom went to the cage, and put her hand in, saying, who wants a ride – and they would walk up her hand, up to her shoulder, so that she could put them into her dressing gown's pockets! That is what they intended. And then there they would sit in her pocket, being ferried to and fro, free of cost, all over the house and garden, talking away and gossiping away merrily, with the human being occasionally adding her own mite to the conversation.

Until father came back home, where they shifted their allegiance to him chirping excitedly, clambering all over his head and shoulders, and pecking at him, telling him what according to them, mom had been doing throughout the day, from their Vantage viewpoint in her pocket, not that they could see anything much through a layer of cotton and semitransparent lace!

Dad still remembers them with lots of fondness. They survived for seven – eight years, which was pretty good going, because the average age is anywhere between five years to 10 years, depending on their state of health.

So whatever you say, these birds are capable are getting under your skin, once you begin to recognize their distinct individuality and personality! That is why you may find your little lovebirds becoming your most dear friends.

My grandfather had six little budgerigars, when I was a child. I remember one time when I was recuperating from measles and was very fractious. He just took those little budgerigars out of their cage, and locked them up in my room. Then he told me to catch them and keep myself occupied, so that for the next four hours, I was busy in this exercise, and not yelling for my grandmother, mother, or grandfather, to sit by my bedside and read out aloud, when they had other more important things to do!

Anyway, this exercise was so good for me; I recovered within the next two days, and was soon back to chirping at my budgerigars in their cage.

So now let us get to know more about this really lovable little bird, and let me tell you one secret. If it is your pet, which you have raised from a baby, it is going to be a really nice source of entertainment, able to mimic the human voice, or any other parrot like capacity.

I remember one of these little pets, which used to hop onto my hand, the moment I poked it into the cage, and then walk right up to my shoulder. After that, it would try its very best to remove the earring from my ear, while chattering in between new attempts to get a new toy, with which to play.

That is why grandma had to remove my studs from my ears and replace them with clipped earrings, so that they could be removed easily by my little friend loudly and triumphantly, without my ear lobe being damaged. But the both of us being babies, at that time, not more than five –six years old, we found these proceedings very entertaining, though an adult would have found it rather trivial, childish, and boring!

As I was less than 10 years old, I was not given the responsibility of taking care of the budgies. A little child cannot take on the care and the feeding of budgies, so that is why, I would suggest you do not gift them to children less than 10 years old, or people, who really do not want to take on the added burden of budgie's care.

This is why I have seen so many budgies being brought to animal shelters, especially the days following Christmas, because these little birds have been gifted to the owners "as cheap" Christmas presents by relatives and friends. And because the gift is free, it is not going to be appreciated.

However, if a child is responsible enough, and old enough to buy a budgie, like any other pet, and buys it out of his or her own pocket money, you know that he is going to take good care of his pet.

This book is for him too, so that he knows how easy or how difficult it is to raise pets.

This story is for him/her. My nephew and niece, when very young kept asking for a dog as a pet, and kept promising that they would take care of the dog. Their mama said that there was no dog to be allowed into the house, because she knew her children. They would go off to school, and she would have to take care of the dog, bathe it, take it to the vet, take it for walks, and be responsible for it.

One day a stray dog entered the house, and the children were very happy with it. They named it Brownie and it lived in the yard. For the first two or three days, the children fed it. Afterwards, they lost interest, and it was only their father who fed it and gave it water.

Some days later, their father had to go away on a weeklong tour. When he came back, Brownie had left the house, because he did not get any food or water, and there was no one to take care of him.

So the next time the children said that they wanted a dog as a pet, their father told them, "You do not deserve a pet. Don't you understand that Brownie had been sent to you to see if you were capable of keeping pets? You lost interest after one week. So Brownie went back and gave his report on you – very lazy children. No use sending a good pet to them, because they are spoiled brats losing interest in what they have and do not appreciate the real thing, when it is right under their noses. Namely me, a dog named Brownie."

So remember, that when you gift your little lovebirds to a person, whether he be 10 or 50, make sure that he is capable of taking care of that precious little gift. And he should cherish that little gift, because this little bird species is going to be a part of his life for the next 5 to 10 years.

You may want to talk about the initial cost, now. There is absolutely no other pet in the World, or even livestock, where the initial cost is so low, especially when maintenance and nest costs are really astonishingly small.

Getting to Know More about Your Lovebird

Budgerigars are astonishingly hardy, because after all, they have been surviving in the Australian outback for millenniums. It can also acclimatize itself to any sort of climate, as long as there is plenty of shade and plenty of water. Frost, rain, or snow is not going to affect it too much, or adversely, as long as it has some occasional sun and fresh air.

So remember that if you want to keep your budgies cooped up in an air-conditioned room, where they do not have fresh air and sun, they are definitely going to start feeling melancholy, and they may wither away.

Also, your budgerigars cannot bear cold wind and fog. So make sure that when and if you raise them in an area, where Blow Blow Thou Winter Wind is common in the winters, you would need safeguards to keep them snug and warm.

Budgies are really prolific breeders, if the conditions are right. On the other hand, canaries are delicate, and good enough as pets, but you cannot use them for breeding for profit.

There is just one point to make sure that your budgerigars are able to raise a happy, healthy family. Leave them strictly alone! Do not interfere with the laying, mating, hatching, feeding, and the rearing of the little babies.

After all, they have been doing this successfully for millenniums in the Australian outback without any of your interference and your looking in, into the nests, to see if any eggs are laid.

Human beings like other peoples' participation in the age old ritual of feeding and bringing up baby. Budgies do not like it, and as you are a human being, and do not understand their language they want to be left alone…be sensible and do exactly that.

Breeding Season

Leave your budgie alone during the breeding season, but begin giving it more green food. You do not need extra food for the babies and for the mother, because the chicks are going to be fed by the food taken by the parents in the crop, and brought up, like pigeons do, whenever they are hungry.

Baby Budgerigars

You do not need to provide vitamins and eggs, and other such brand-name foods which are being sold in the market as budgie food.

But as my aunt told me, the more birds you keep, the more the costs are reduced, because wholesale dealers are going to give you larger amounts of food, at a much lower rate.

You are going to begin small, just by buying a pair. Make sure that they are a male and female, and if they are in different colors, so much the better. An experienced breeder is going to sell you a pair, instead of just two male budgies, or female budgies. They are going to talk, talk, talk, all the while, while you are waiting for them to raise a family!

These birds are capable of going into nesting up to 5 to 6 times in one breeding season. So if you have them raising two little chicks, successfully each season, you have 12 healthy little baby birds.

You can keep four and sell eight. And with the money you got from those eight, you can build more cages.

Male or female budgie?

When I asked my budgies' raising friend how she knew whether her budgies were males or females, she said, well, if the budgie lays eggs, it is a female, in a really my dear Watson, how dumb you are, tone. Haha, I obviously did not think.

That is because the male budgies also sit on the nest to keep them warm. So unless she picked up the budgie, and marked it with indelible ink, she would have to find other ways with which to prove that a budgie was a male or a female.

When I stopped belaboring her with a pillow and she stopped hooting with laughter I found this URL, which tells you how you can recognize a male or a female budgie, from its cere, which is just above the beak and you can call it a nose, because the nostrils are there.

http://www.birds-online.de/allgemein/geschlecht_en.htm

Also, if you have birds in your cage, the bird which is social, talkative, even say some words, and comes to meet you, at the cage wall wire, whenever you approach the cage, is quite possibly a male. Female birds are more timid. They may grow a bit aggressive during the breeding season, but if they are not breeding, they are going to be quiet.

The male bird is the one which keeps tapping, trying to talk to you, and showing off more. Try placing him in a nest, with a more timid bird, which you have recognized as a female.

If there is no nest in the cage, the female is not going to lay any eggs. So remember that they should be well provided with nests, which can be enough of an opening into which the bird can enter, and enough space into which it can make itself comfortable and raise its babies.

My aunt of course had a number of empty earthenware pots hung up on all the walls of the cage, with sturdy wire in order to make the budgie feel that it was making a nest, in a hole, high up in a eucalyptus tree, far away from dingo or any other predatory bird or animal attack.

Also, she placed some earthenware pots on the floor of the cage. For 15 bird pairs, she had 15 pots. They were not huge ones. That is because if your budgie thinks that the hole is huge, and which allows a large animal to enter, and gobble up the whole family, the pot is not going to be used for nesting.

If you intend to breed them, you will like your pair to raise just two or three nests successfully, so that the hen can stay healthy, feeding her chicks. From three nests, if the raising has been done successfully, you can get up to 15 chicks.

A coconut has been used to make a comfortable nest for this budgie.

That means expanding your cage! So unless you decide to sell all your young and start new each season with a single pair of birds, you have to look at ways in which to expand your cage size as well as your business. The first successful season is going to have you hooked as well as feeling triumphant!

Different Colors of Budgies

More and more color combinations are being found, as different strains are being bred, so you can find really amazing color combinations, all brought about through experimentation or just by chance.

By the way, you may want to ask a friend who does not know anything about birds and parrots, the color of a parrot. His immediate reaction is going to be green, of course, shouldn't it be green? That is because all parrots – the grown-up ones squawking all over your fruit trees – are green, with red beaks. And that is why shopkeepers take advantage of this little bit of ignorance, and tell them that they are going to give you a rare little bird, at a very reasonable rate. And then they asked the earth as its price, this deal done only for you, because you are such a good customer.

It is when you go to a friend's house at the other corner of the town, and find that he has bought a pair in that same color – really quite common, wouldn't you know – for less than a couple of dollars or pounds or euros, you come home steaming and take out all your anger on that poor little budgie, for no fault of its own. And you may even start to neglect it or give it away to the nearest animal shelter.

So remember that there is a tremendously large range of colors, and they are definitely not rare!

So remember that even though green is the basic and original natural color thanks to different breeding experiments all over the world, lovebirds have a large variety and range in colors and shades. So here are some of the common colors, which are normally found in budgies and easily available.

Greens – Olive, dark, and light green, olive with gray wings, or with yellow wings.

Yellow– yellow olive, dark yellow, and light yellow.

Blue – sky and cobalt blue, violet, and even mauve.

Sky-blue with a little bit of light and deep white, and violet with a little bit of cobalt blue. As for the wings, they can be yellow, light green, olive green, and dark green. Gray wings, cobalt blue, sky blue, light green, olive, dark green, gray green, violet, and also all gray.

Albinos are pure white, but their eyes are pink. In the same way, Lutinos, which are definitely not found in nature, are pure yellow with pink eyes. They are actually albinos and they should not be confused with the original yellow colored ones, which are going to have dark or black colored eyes.

You can also get cinnamon wings, gray, gray green, sky-blue and cobalt, dark green and olive combinations. Gray wings can be light, dark, or medium colored, with light green, dark green, and olive combinations…

One can make a list of all the available combinations, even though I have not seen red making a very prominent appearance in budgies, even though there are other parrot species with plenty of red feathers.

Let me tell you about another color range – these are called the Opalines.

Here, you are going to see green birds with masks on their faces, colored buttercup yellow. The masks are going to be white in the blue, gray, mauve, and violet opalines. The color combinations in opalines are also dark, and light green, gray green, gray, violet, sky-blue, olive green, and mauve.

See the v shape between the wings of this budgie that is a characteristic of an Opaline.

This mask is going to extend over the head area, and is going to march into the body. It is going to be level with the butt of iridescent and body colored wings. The undulations which are wavy and very attractive are going to stop at those points. So that means you are going to have a clear effect shaped like a V, right in between the top of your budgie's wings.

Choosing the Perfect Budgie Specimen

So how do you recognize a good specimen of a budgerigar, when you are stocking up your stock?

If you know all about these basic tips, to choose a high quality budgerigar, you can buy a specimen, which is above or up to standard. That is because good stock is necessary in order to begin your breeding operations, for a successful progress of your small business.

Believe it or not, many pet shop owners do not know whether a bird is of high quality or of low quality. They just want to sell their birds at a profit. So if you buy 20 or 30 bird there is just a chance that one or two of them are going to be of higher quality than the rest. A good budgerigar is proud instance, when it is sitting on its perch, with a body tapering gracefully from the neck to the tip of the tail. The line from the tail to the neck is going to be as nearly straight as can be. The length of a healthy and good bird should be about 8 ½ inches. If you have an 8 ½ inches bird, you have an excellent specimen.

Then look at the bird sitting on its perch. Are the wings crossed? Do not buy that bird, however pretty you find the color combination. However, if the bird has crossed its wings temporarily, which is just temporary, and occurs when the bird has just alighted from its flight, and needs a little bit of time to balance itself on a steady support, the wings will be crossed for a little while. When it is at rest, and possibly telling you of all the great and glorious things it has done, both the wings should be on its sides, with the wingtips just touching each other.

The eyes have to be bright, eager, enthusiastic, and set away from the top of the budgie's skull. The skull curvature should be bold. The head should be wide and round.

The color should be consistent and clear. The feathers should be healthy looking, not molting – except in the molting season – and the plumage should be bright and attractive.

The masks should be wide and deep. There should be six large spots which are evenly distributed at the throat. There should also be a cheek patch, on each side, which should be large and bold.

These are just some of the points, which can help you buy a good bird specimen. Also, go by instinct. Let me give you an example of instinct. This was not for a bird, but for a dog, in a dog exhibition, about nine years ago.

During an annual dog show, in our city, I just was part of the spectators, watching the beautiful, well groomed, and well-trained dogs being shown around the ring by their trainers. There was one she dog, who was a cut above the rest, with her head up straight, her form excellent, well trained, her eyes bright. I just kept watching her and then said, number five that is the best one of the lot.

Unfortunately, the judges had already made up their minds, and did not bother about number five. After the results had been given, a spectator right next to me asked me whether I had been breeding dogs. I said of course not. Then he asked how I knew that number five was the best. I said, "Sir, if the judges cannot recognize quality when they see it, I am not anybody to tell them." Two minutes later, number five was brought back into the exhibition rink. And she was exhibited along with the winner. And everybody could see that number five was a cut above the rest. Afterwards, all those people who had heard me say that number five was the best asked me whether I was associated with that particular kennel. I said "Never heard of it before, nor have I seen that dog before. But just look at her." And they looked.

She was given the much-deserved prize of best trained dog in the all comers' class! That is because a person who knows and loves dogs has an instinct for the best quality. So allow your instinct to work.

Housing for Your Birdies

Firstly, you have to know the priorities of space and finances before you begin to look at the housing for your birds. My father did not spend any money in building expensive cages, when he kept his birds. He just made a frame, of four pieces of sturdy wood, nailed them together, and nailed wire gauge netting all over the frame.

There are plenty of DIY projects, out there, which can help you make your own cages, keeping in view, your available space and your finances. Remember that your birds need plenty of space in which to fly. They should also have sunlight and fresh air. That is because ultraviolet rays are necessary to keep them happy. That is why in places like the UK, where sunshine is not so common, when compared to countries like Australia and the Mediterranean countries, budgies do not do very well. They need their daily dose of vitamin D.

Also, the shelter should also have an area which should be well covered, apart from being well ventilated and warm, especially during the winter season.

Aunty brought her birds indoors, during the winter, especially as this area is subject to frost and harsh winter winds, especially in December and January. When I asked her why she did not keep each pair separated, she said that it was good for the hens and the cocks to choose their own mates, through natural and innate instinctive selection.

Remember that your birds may look little, but they are very powerful and strong fliers. They cannot be cooped up in a small cage. They need plenty of exercise throughout the day. Remember to provide the cage with more nest boxes than there are birds, because you want them to choose what they like and in which they feel safe and secure.

The boxes should all be hung up at the same height, because budgerigars are always going to go for the highest box, and are going to quarrel for the privilege of nesting in it!

Also, the number of cocks should be equal to the number of hens. People who try selective breeding with just one pair are going to find the resulting birds of a much lower quality, because the pair have not had an opportunity to choose their own partners. Naturally, the gene line is not going to be strong as it is in nature.

Advantages of Making Your Own Cages

When you make your own cages, you can make them to suit your own purpose. Wire cages which are completely open are not recommended.

If you have some money to spare, you can either make fronts made out of bars which have been punched out with openings, for water or for seed containers. These are expensive to buy. If you are a DIY type of person, make your own front of half inch wire mesh, measuring 36 inches to 18 inches for the largest, and other measurements in between, depending.

A large cage should be 48 inches long, 22 inches wide, and 22 inches in height. This is the practical maximum. However, you can diminish the size depending on your requirements.

The back, top, bottom portion, and the sides are going to be covered with good hardwood. This is fixed to a sturdy wooden framework. Hardwood is warm and cheaper. The front is going to be open and have a door from which the bird can enter into the nest and you can see into the nest, through the wire mesh. There should be two perches at different heights.

Here is the basic frame design for a nesting box.

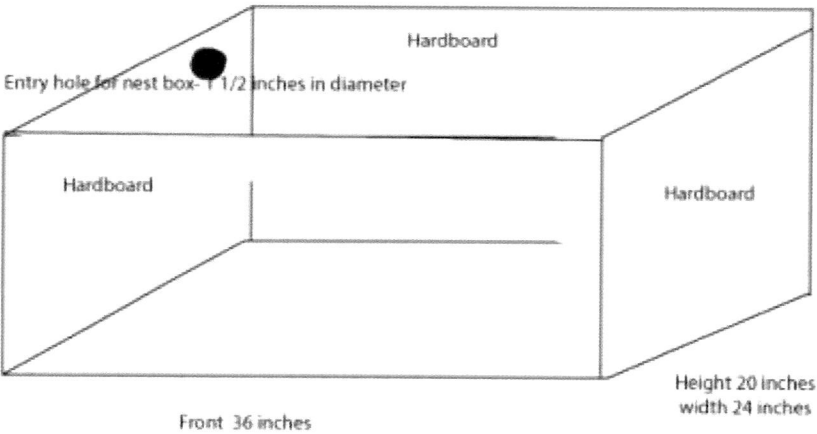

Framework for nesting box.

The nest box should be roomy enough for the bird to raise a family. Two doors mean that the birds can come and go as they please.

You can put this nesting box in the aviary, once you know that a pair is ready to raise a family. Remember, if there is no nest, there is not going to be any pairing or mating. The cocks look for the best nests and fight over them. So you should have enough nests that and all of them hanging at the same height, so that there is no sudden death!

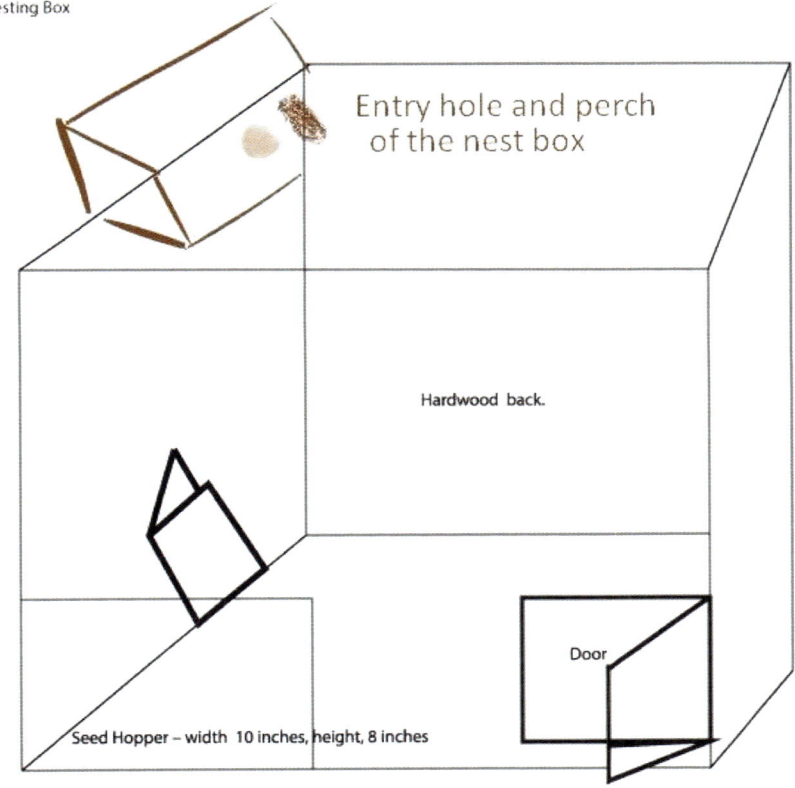

Height of box – 20 inches. Width of box – 24 inches
Seed hopper for feed – Height 8 inches, width 10 "

If you have a number of birds and have plenty of bird room available, you may want to make these nesting boxes the way one makes a chest of drawers, in tiers, and layers upon layers. You will be saving a lot of space and material, if you make your nesting boxes in this manner, because the top of one box is going to be the bottom portion of the other box.

That means a really compact nesting area for all your birds. And also, it is so easy to transport from one place to another.

This DIY project is going to take a little bit of your time. That is why; I suggest looking for other natural nests, like they do in places, where there are lots of clay pots, coconuts, letterboxes, and any other square and sturdy boxes, which have a small opening.

If you are looking for letterboxes, make sure that they are not made of metal. You do not want your little birdies suffering in high-temperatures, when the metal warms up, do you? I once walked into a metal storage room/canister in the summer, and the temperature in it was astonishingly, 7 to 10° more than outdoors. And it was just early morning. In the summer, it would have been a melting pot for any who dared enter.

Tier boxes

When you are building tiers of cages, you can construct the floor of each with half an inch wire mesh. That means you can raise the bottom cages, 2 feet from the ground. This way all the dirt is going to drop right through the mesh, from the top to the bottom, without you having to clean out the cages every single day. We just need to sweep from under the lowermost cage with a dustpan and brush in less than a minute, every day.

Your birds are definitely not going to have any problem with the wire mesh, because you can see them clinging on the mesh, in the flight area, and telling all the other birds inside the aviary, about what those human beings are doing out in the garden right now.

You may say that the birds living in the lowermost nesting box are going to have a tough time, what with all the droppings from above falling down, but surprisingly enough, it is not so. These birds have a cage, which is as clean or as dirty as that of the cages above! You can also, along with the seed hopper, place a solid and narrow shelf, at the back of each cage, in which you are going to place water containers, pieces of grit – little birds need grit, so that the seeds can be ground together in their crops – and also powdered bone meal for the protein. This shelf, which is about 4 inches wide, is excellent for those little extras, which will help keep your birdies happy.

You do not need a seed hopper, if you intend to change the seed and water every day by hand. However, few of us have this inclination, time or energy to do that. We would rather fill up the seed box, and allow the bird to eat.

You can make a very satisfactory and useful seed hopper, which is going to have enough seed for all the birds to have lots of meals for a number of weeks.

The seed hopper is going to be fixed to the cage, either to the side, or in the front, with an opening being cut in the hard board of the cage or in the wire mesh. Naturally, it is going to be of any size you please.

It is going to be a box, with a base, back, two sides, but the top is going to be hinged. There is not going to be any front, because your birds need easy access to their seed. A piece of plywood is fixed at an angle, and below it, coming back at an angle and another piece of plywood with a raised edge pinned to it. There is going to be a ¼ inch wide gap between the two sloping pieces of wood. This means the seed, which is poured into a triangular space formed by the large sloping piece and the back and sides of the hopper will filter down into the tray.

The raised edge is going to prevent the seed from sliding down to the base of the hopper.

Just put a movable tray, this does not need to have any edges and which you can pull in and out under the seed tray. This is made up of plywood, cut to fit.

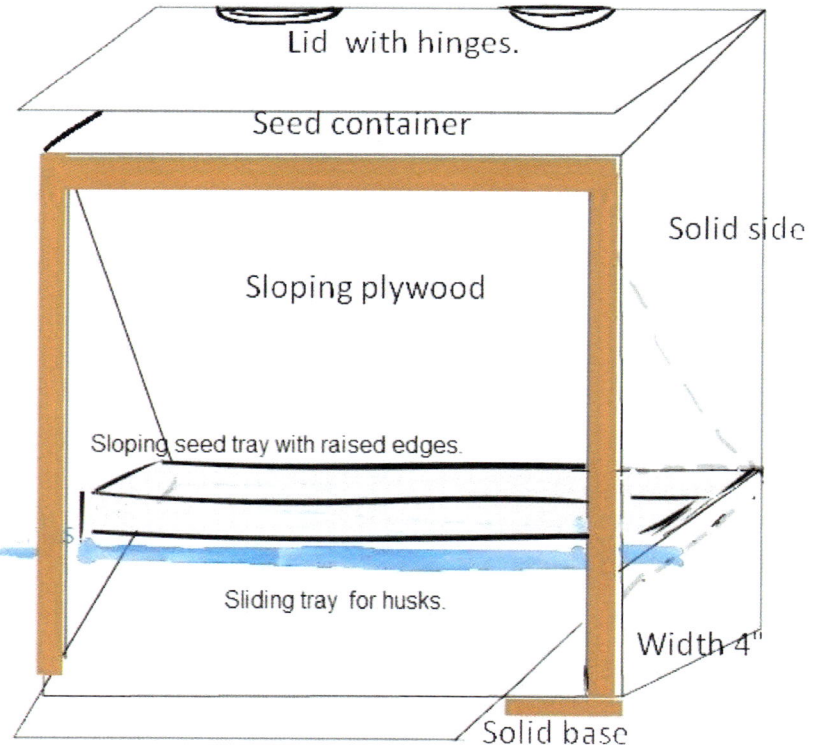

There should be a 1-4 inches gap between the sloping plywood and the sloping seed tray. This is to enable the seeds to slide into the seed tray.

Your bird is going to have a place on which to perch, between the sides and just below the tray. So when your bird is dining off these seeds, the seed husk is dropped onto the tray. The removable tray can be removed, every now and then, and the waste husks disposed of.

Try your hand at making out this seed hopper right now, according to the sketch. The height is 8 inches and the width is 10 inches.

Drinking water fount

It is very easy to make a drinking water fount, even though larger founts are available in the market for poultry. You just need a metal tray. Along with that, you need a round collar. The collar should be higher than the edge of the tray. It should be soldered in the center.

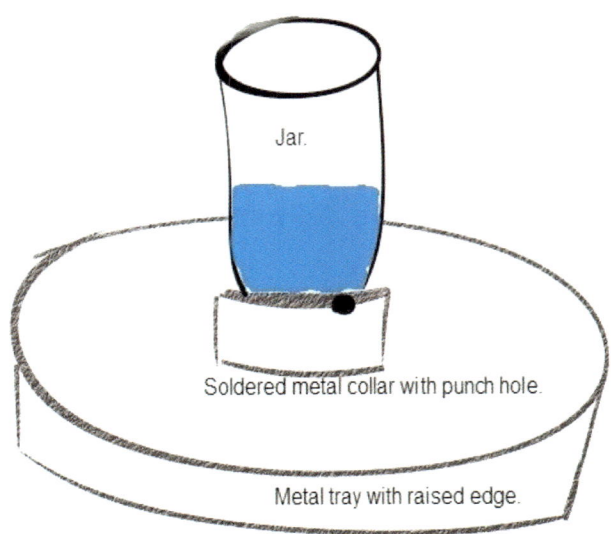

Punch a hole in the collar. It should be just a fraction under the height of the outside edge of the tray.

The collar should be of such a size, that it snugly fits the inverted neck of a jam jar. If you fill up the jar with water, and placed the tray upside down on it, the collar coming just to the shoulder of the jar and then turn it over, you are going to find water automatically filling the rest of the tray through the hole.

And as the water is consumed, more water is going to take its place until the jar is empty again. Then you can refill the jam bottle. This means that you are always going to have a clean water supply for your birds.

There has to be one point to mind, when you use wire mesh. Any cut ends, which may injure your birds, should be covered with thin plywood.

Diet for your birds

The staple diet for your birds is going to be birdseed, which is a mixture of millet and canary seed. You may find some shops selling you budgerigar mixture, but if you can get quality material, get some canary seed and millet. These should be mixed up with an equal parts proportion, and when there are youngsters around, add oats. Add 10% to your seed mixture.

You can also add a little bit of linseed, which is going to affect the coats of your bird. This oil is essential, especially during the molding season. Budgies really do not like linseed much because it is fattening. So you are going to give it in small amounts to caged birds, only when they are molting.

You can also place sprays of millet in cages and aviaries. That is because cereal seeds in nature are normally found on stalks, on which little birds can perch and off which they can feed.

Budgies enjoy these sprays, so if you can find them easily, your budgies are going to find plenty of entertainment just swinging on these sprays.

Before your birds start mating, just add a little bit of cod liver oil and also in the winter, to the seeds. Not more than one teaspoonful for every pint.

Remember that these budgies have been around for centuries, without vitamins, proteins, and all the extras being marketed by people who want to sell you budgies.

Vitamins are necessary for every living thing, but good seed mixtures are going to give your birds all the nourishment they need.

If you can find chickweed in the garden, give them to your birds. They like it very much. Also, your birds are going to be more fertile, if you give them this every other day. Get them from your own garden. Dry these plants, before you give them to your birds. Also, dandelions. These should be given just once a week. Shepherds purse, spinach, and lettuce tops, roots of spinach, and carrot tops are also good greens. But do not give greens at any time, in very large quantity. Give them a little, regularly.

Grit is very essential for the birds. Sand which you get in pet shops does not have enough grit, so just buy it separately and place a little bit in your cage.

Many people have the idea that birds need to be fed twice a day, but that is not so with budgies. Feed has to be available the whole time. Never allow the containers to become empty. And also water. One day without food and water and you are going to lose your budgies.

Management of Your Birds

Cleaning out of the cages is necessary and if you cannot manage it every day, at least you should do it every second day. But when the chickens are being reared or are out of the cage, you will need to clean them every day, otherwise you are going to have budgie odor in the area.

When cleaning out the cages, you just need to remove any removable trays, throw away the debris and renew the sand. Every week, just wipe the perches with a cloth, which has just been damped with a little bit of mild antiseptic. Birds really do not like the smell of antiseptic, so do not use it very often.

Also, please DO NOT over crowd your cage with birds

Sometimes, you may need to catch your little bird to inspect it. Do not ever use an ordinary fishnet, because the wire is very coarse.

Make a wireframe, 12 inches in diameter, with a short handle. If you have a longer handle, it is going to get tangled up with the perches. Use soft fine textured cloth for the net. When you are trying to catch it, do not do any excited swiping. Wait for it to settle down on the wire mesh. Then capture it. Swiping at it, when it is in flight, is going to scare it and excite it. You do not want to terrify your birds, do you?

Ventilation should be adequate, and you should make sure that they are protected from harsh weather – sun and the cold. My aunt's large aviary, is under the shade of a huge tree. The birds do not mind occasional insects falling down from the tree, right into the cage either!

Also, they enjoy the raindrops, pattering down the leaves, and I have seen them enjoying the rainfall/shower, when it is light. It does not rain very heavily in our area, so the birds are never at the mercy of heavy downpours.

Remember that the birds should never get themselves wet, especially in the late afternoon or in the evening, so if there are chances of heavy rain, cover up the cages, with a covering.

If you keep poultry, you know all about their specific molting season, but budgies do not molt at any given or fixed time. The first molt for your chickens is always going to be when they are three months old. If they cast a lot of feathers, there is a chance that they are going to catch a chill so keep an eye open for these birds.

Put them into covered quarters. Chickens are going to get their deeper adults shades, in three months, losing the baby down.

There is always the problem of varmints, especially rats, when food is around. Also, rats like budgerigars as a change in diet. So that is why, make sure your aviary is raised to a safe height. My aunt's aviary is one and a half feet above the ground.

The light in your aviary should not be very bright, if you want some light in the nighttime. They enjoy a little bit of light, just about the brightness of torchlight. Also, when they are going to roost, or they are roosting, do not disturb them. If you have to disturb them, move very quietly, with slow movements, and dim lights. But do not enter the cage after dark or after they have roosted. This is going to terrify them, and they are going to fly into a panic. And then there is a chance of them hurting themselves, by hitting the wire mesh or even against the walls.

Selective breeding is a very extensive topic, which needs plenty of experience and knowledge. So I am not touching on this particular subject in this book, at the moment. But green is the original and basic color of the species they have higher physical standards than other colors. That is why green is always the basis of breeding, mating them with other colors so that you can get stronger physical qualities in the strain. Here, of course, common sense, power of observation, experience, and instinct comes into play, especially when you are experimenting. But nature does not like this sort of experimentation, so if you have got a good result, make sure that you have recorded them for future reference.

Baby Chicks

When you are breeding two birds, the main factors are readiness for breeding and good health. Good health is seen in the brightness of the plumage, alertness, activity, and then you can look at the cere. The hen's cere is going to be fawn in color. The cock's cere is blue. This is one indication that the birds are ready to mate.

The mating season can be any time in nature, but you as a breeder can begin from March and April. Early breeding means that the first molding is going to be done in sunny weather. Those which are born later in the season are going to be exposed to colder weather.

The hen should at least be 11 months old and the cock around 10 months old. How long are they going to breed and up to what age, is going to depend on the health of the birds. The hens can breed until they are three years old and the cocks until they are six years old. The birds should not be older than that.

So how are you going to know that the bird is ready for nesting? They normally make their nests in a flat place, and once you see the hen bird entering her nest very often, that is an indication that she is ready to lay her eggs. If they have been a fortnight together and you cannot see any indications of her eagerness to lie, it seems like the pair do not fancy each other.

They lay every alternate day. The hatching is also done every alternate day. The hen may not sit on the first egg. The first two chicks may be born with just one day in between. When there is a large clutch, the last chick may be at a disadvantage. That is because the largest chick is going to try to feed itself first. That is why the smallest chick may not grow swiftly and satisfactorily.

So here are some steps, which can help chicks from one clutch to grow healthy and swiftly. Foster parents do not object to little chicks being introduced in their nests.

Also, if you think that the parents are going to get disturbed, when you open up the cage and the nest boxes to see the progress of the eggs and the chicks, if they are used to you, they might make a noise, but they do not really mind. They know you as their source of feed, water, entertainment, and protection.

A periodical inspection is necessary so that you can know which eggs are infertile, and they can be taken away. You can also check to see if the birds are healthy. Once every day is all right and necessary. Nest boxes which have been fixed to the sides of the cages can be opened up easily, without disturbing your birds too much.

During the incubation, do not do any cleaning or changing of the nest boxes. Wait until all the eggs are hatched. After hatching, you will need to clean regularly.

I would suggest changing instead. Put the chicks into a cardboard box. Make sure that they are not cold. Clean the nest box thoroughly and then put the chicks back.

Remember to keep a record of your chicks' pedigrees. Each box should have a serial number.

Your record should have a description of both the parents and their numbers, if you have numbered them.

1. The date in which they were put in the box.
2. The date of the first egg.
3. The date on which the first chick was expected to hatch, and the date when it hatched.
4. Number of eggs in the clutch.
5. Number of the chicks hatched.
6. Any other remarks, especially characteristics of the parents as exhibited during the breeding and the rearing of the chicks.

These records are necessary, because you cannot remember all the details mentally. These sheets are also going to tell you all about the number of infertile eggs. Thanks to these records, you are also going to know when the eggs are expected to hatch, and when they hatch in reality.

Incubation is normally for 18 days. Allow 21 days for the eggs, and at the end of this time, the ones which are not hatched are considered to be infertile.

However, during the sitting period, you can see the embryo forming as a dark patch/shadow in the egg. Nevertheless, do not make a guess on whether an egg is fertile or not, and allow all the eggs to remain in the nest until all the chicks are hatched.

Sometimes the parents do not know that the chicks have to be fed after they have been hatched. So put them immediately into a foster parent's nest and hope that the parents are going to learn some sense with the next brood.

To know that your chicks are fed properly, after they have been hatched, open the nest box – a hinged opening is excellent, and looks at the crop. If the crop is bulging from outside the neck area that means it has been fed.

Any chicks which are neglected have to be transferred immediately, within 12 hours of being hatched. But if the crops are bulging, you do not need to worry at all. Once the birds start feeding their chicks, they are not going to neglect them ever.

Also, foster parents can only be there, when you have two or more pairs breeding at the same time. That means you have extra pairs standing by, so that you can transfer to their nest boxes any chicks, or even eggs from other boxes if necessary.

This is only going to be necessary when you are breeding on a very large scale. But you are going to be surprised how fast your stock grows! That is why you might find a number of pairs breeding at the same time.

The chicks are going to begin to leave the nest, about 30 days after they had hatched. The parents are going to feed them, if they want for a little while, but the chicks are going to fend for themselves, instinctively and naturally. Leave the chicks with the parents for about a week watching them carefully to make sure that they are able to feed themselves. After that, you can transfer them to another nursery aviary, where you can keep your eye on them. This is, of course, when you are dealing with lots and lots of chicks and breeding pairs.

Your budgies are very adventurous, but there might be some, who do not want to leave the nest. You will have to remove them, especially when the hen is ready for her second clutch and is ready to lay and hatch another brood within the same season.

That means the chicks have to be taken out – they are ready to leave the nest, but do not really bother about that activity or think about it seriously – and they can be placed with other birds that will take care of them.

However, if you do not want another clutch, just remove the eggs, and allow the babies to enjoy some more quality time with their parents. It is very entertaining to see the parents teaching their children how to fly. I saw one not so adventurous baby bird being pushed off the perch by his father! My ensuing roar of laughter, brought back an indignant chirp, but that little chick and I became quite good friends in a couple of days. It being a male, used to come flying to the wire mesh, whenever I came to visit – I lived just a couple of houses away from my aunt at that time, and visiting was quite often – and we used to talk to each other for quite a long time.

If your hen tends to more than four or five nests in one season, discourage her by closing up the nest box or taking it into an area, where there are no nest boxes. You can also remove the eggs. You might think this to be a waste, but in the longer run; it is a good option, especially when this is the last clutch. You do not want to tire a good layer out, do you?

For a nursery cage, put a number of chicks together and watch them carefully. Remember that there is always the chance of disappointment, but as they are so prolific, dead chicks and unfertile eggs should never be a matter of stress and strain. Unless, of course you were expecting too much of one particular clutch in terms of genealogical strength and color combination.

Marketing your birds

There is always going to be a great demand for your birds, as pets, and as breeding stock, especially if you are known to be an experienced and good breeder. Surplus stock can easily be sold in a number of outlets. These can either be in your city, or you can even transport them.

For transporting your birds, put them in a box. Do not put them on perches. Make sure the box is well padded. There should be adequate food and water for them. Label the box carefully as livestock.

Along with this, there are going to be individual requests, requests from friends and neighbors, especially through word-of-mouth, and also demands, in case you have done some advertising in the local papers.

They are also going to be a large number of unsolicited requests. If you have the stock and you want to sell, you can do so. Pet shops may possibly require a steady supply of birds, so if you have surplus, you can always give them to your local pet shops.

Obviously, when you are supplying to your pet shops, you may not make as much of a profit, as when you are selling to individual customers. But then pet shops are a business. And if you have a reputation of being reliable, for a fixed amount of birds which are healthy and of good stock, you can also get a contract.

Start small. If you have a large surplus, you can do a bit of advertising. Make sure that these birds can be viewed easily by your customers, when they come to visit your garden/aviary. Salesmanship is more of looking for the best time to sell. That is, of course, the holiday season, when you are going to get a higher price for gifts for kids.

Once you have segregated the birds you want to sell, you are going to do the pricing according to the records. Study their details, and then you can set your own price. Add the price to the cards, so that the buyer knows how much he needs to pay for a really good pair of budgies.

Also, keep the breeding cards ready, so that the purchaser knows that the stock is healthy, and genealogically sound. You can also talk about the characteristics of the birds and their pedigree, briefly, to the buyer. And this is going to show him that you know your birds because you have taken the trouble to provide him with proof of its origin, the care, the skill, and other factors, which helped him make up his mind to buy your birds.

Pet shops do not care much about pedigrees. You may also want to make a file of the birds sold, when, and to whom, for future reference. Also, if a buyer wants a particular bird, he is going to be very well pleased, if you contact him and tell him, well, you were looking for a yellow bird with purple feathers, well, you would like to come visit it, yes? More often than not, he is going to come and visit!

Diseases and Treatment

You are fortunate that these birds are very hardy, and rarely succumb to diseases and infections, if you are careful. Nevertheless, prevention is always much better than cure. And if you find a little bird ailing, quarantine it immediately. I am talking in clichés here, but a stitch in time saves nine. A bird which is sickly is going to droop, and lose all enthusiasm. The feathers will be held loosely. Imagine that you are sickening for flu. How do you feel?

Look at your birds. Does one remotely look like that, lethargic, with no energy, and so on? Do not take any chances. Isolate that bird immediately. Bad physical housing conditions, lack of cleanliness, and exposure to bad weather are factors which are going to promote mild and possibly serious infections in your birds.

Place your bird in its hospital cage. This is a cage, which is warmed, or you can just put it in a warm room. If it is suffering from a chill, it is going to perk up wonderfully. But if it is sick with a serious infection, this warmth may not have any effect at all. Also, warmth can prevent a slight chill from developing into serious problems like bronchitis.

Birds being reared in harsh conditions are prone to bronchitis and pneumonia, like human beings.

My grandfather found one of his little birdies– it was named Birdie – sick, so grandma told him, if Brandy perks you up in the winter, it should do the same to your buddy! So he took a teaspoonful of Brandy and put it in warm water. Then he took the bird carefully in his hand, and squeezed it very, very gently. The bird opened its beak, an eyedropper was inserted immediately and a couple of drops fed to little birdie. This diluted spirit is wonderful as a stimulant, especially in the winter. You can also give it drops of warm milk.

The only problem, to our great amusement was that that little birdie decided to become a confirmed dipso. He loved brandy water! He needed one drop of diluted Brandy every day, and whenever grandfather came to his cage, even if he was fluttering about before and flying around, he would immediately start his drooping and making sad little noises.

Grandpa had to get it out, and talk to it. But it was not having any small talk ever, until it got its evening tipple, in the winter.

Birdie soon became a top favorite at get-togethers and parties, when he was taken out of his cage, and given a very little bit of Brandy diluted a lot in warm water. It literally got tipsy, and even though the ladies protested, the gents loved its antics. Especially when it could not walk a straight line, or when it went off to sleep with a feeble chirp. By the way, it never suffered from a hangover, and next morning, it was very chirpy, calling for grandfather.

It being a male talked. And it used to mimic my voice, calling Grand-paaa. It lived until the age of 10, and grandpa said that it was all that Brandy! It was an excellent specimen.

There is another common disease, called enteric. Just like human beings, if you find birds suffering from loose bowels, put them in a cage, where you are not going to give it any food or water or stimulant for the next 12 to 24 hours. This is going to clear its system. If human beings can be cured with this standard treatment, so can birds, including budgies.

Rheumatism is one not so common ailment and it prevents your bird from perching. It is going to stick to the wire mesh, or just remain on the ground.

If you pick it up, and inspect its feet you are going to see that the claws do not open properly.

Place the bird in a small cage. Allow it to plunge its feet into a diluted iodine bath twice a day. Keep the foot in for two or three minutes at the most. The rheumatism is going to go away within the week.

The main causes of diseases is a weakening of stock, due to deficiency in nourishment, intensive inbreeding, which weakens the gene lines and bad housing conditions.

Like I said before, prevention is always far, far better than attempting any cure, so if you are buying some stock, from some unknown agency, you would want to quarantine it for some time, before you introduce it into your aviary.

Conclusion

This book has given you some basic information, which you may find interesting, especially if you want to know more about budgies, their care, and breeding. The topic is extensive, so you may want to go online to look for ways to exhibit your budgies, the budgie market, and even new color combinations coming out, reared by enthusiastic breeders.

There might be a budgie club in your city. If you do not have it, why not start one?

There are a number of budgie societies all over the World today, online and in large towns. So get on to some forums, snap some pictures of your budgies, and post them online. You are going to find thousands of enthusiasts out there, willing to inform you about tips and techniques in budgie care. You are also going to get to know all about new markets, especially if you are thinking up breeding budgies as a small business.

You can also get tips on how to make free flight aviaries, but the idea of setting them free, so that they can come back to roost is not one which I would advise. That is because a budgie tasting liberty for the first time is definitely going to get confused and it is possible that you may lose it. Also, if there is any change in weather, your budgie might get caught out in the rain or winds. So that little bird is lost.

So enjoy this new hobby, which may turn out to be a lucrative small business for you. The more you learn about your birds, the more engrossed you are going to get in rearing them. So enjoy your feathered friends.

Live Long and Prosper!

Author Bio

Dueep Jyot Singh is a Management and IT Professional who managed to gather Postgraduate qualifications in Management and English and Degrees in Science, French and Education while pursuing different enjoyable career options like being an hospital administrator, IT,SEO and HRD Database Manager/ trainer, movie , radio and TV scriptwriter, theatre artiste and public speaker, lecturer in French, Marketing and Advertising, ex-Editor of Hearts On Fire (now known as Solstice) Books Missouri USA, advice columnist and cartoonist, publisher and Aviation School trainer, ex-moderator on Medico.in, banker, student councilor ,travelogue writer … among other things!

One fine morning, she decided that she had enough of killing herself by Degrees and went back to her first love -- writing. It's more enjoyable! She already has 48 published academic and 14 fiction- in- different- genre books under her belt.

When she is not designing websites or making Graphic design illustrations for clients , she is browsing through old bookshops hunting for treasures, of which she has an enviable collection – including R.L. Stevenson, O.Henry, Dornford Yates, Maurice Walsh, De Maupassant, Victor Hugo, Sapper, C.N. Williamson, "Bartimeus" and the crown of her collection- Dickens "The Old Curiosity Shop," and "Martin Chuzzlewit" and so on… Just call her "Renaissance Woman" - collecting herbal remedies, acting like Universal Helping Hand/Agony Aunt, or escaping to her dear mountains for a bit of exploring, collecting herbs and plants, and trekking.

Check out some of the other JD-Biz Publishing books

[Gardening Series on Amazon](#)

Download Free Books!

http://MendonCottageBooks.com

Health Learning Series

Country Life Books

GRANDMA'S
NATURAL REMEDIES
AND ANCIENT HERBAL
BEAUTY RECIPES
Volume 1
HEALTH LEARNING SERIES
DUEEP J SINGH AND J DAVIDSON
GRANDMA'S
NATURAL REMEDIES
AND ANCIENT HERBAL
BEAUTY RECIPES
Volume 2
HEALTH LEARNING SERIES
DUEEP J SINGH AND J DAVIDSON
GRANDMA'S
NATURAL REMEDIES
AND ANCIENT RECIPES
GRANDMA'S CURE FOR OBESITY
GRANDMA'S CURE FOR THE COMMON COLD
Volume 3
HEALTH LEARNING SERIES
DUEEP J SINGH AND J DAVIDSON
GRANDMA'S
NATURAL REMEDIES AND
ANCIENT HERBAL RECIPES
Volume 4
HEALTH LEARNING SERIES
DUEEP J SINGH AND J DAVIDSON
GRANDMA'S
HERBAL LORE
ANCIENT HERBAL RECIPES AND REMEDIES
Volume 5
HEALTH LEARNING SERIES
DUEEP J SINGH AND J DAVIDSON
GRANDMA'S
ANCIENT
BEAUTY REMEDIES
FROM HER KITCHEN
Volume 6
HEALTH LEARNING SERIES
DUEEP J SINGH AND J DAVIDSON
GRANDMA'S
EASY TO USE TIPS
IN THE KITCHEN AND OUTDOORS
Volume 7
HEALTH LEARNING SERIES
DUEEP J SINGH AND J DAVIDSON
GRANDMA'S
HOUSEHOLD HINTS AND RECIPES
USING TIME TESTED
ECONOMICAL TIPS IN YOUR HOME
75 Tips
Remove Stains
Peel Tomatoes
Perfect Pies
HEALTH LEARNING SERIES
DUEEP J SINGH AND J DAVIDSON
GRANDMA'S
NATURAL REMEDIES
AND ANCIENT RECIPES
ALL 5 BOOKS IN 1
HEALTH LEARNING SERIES
DUEEP J SINGH AND J DAVIDSON

Health Learning Series

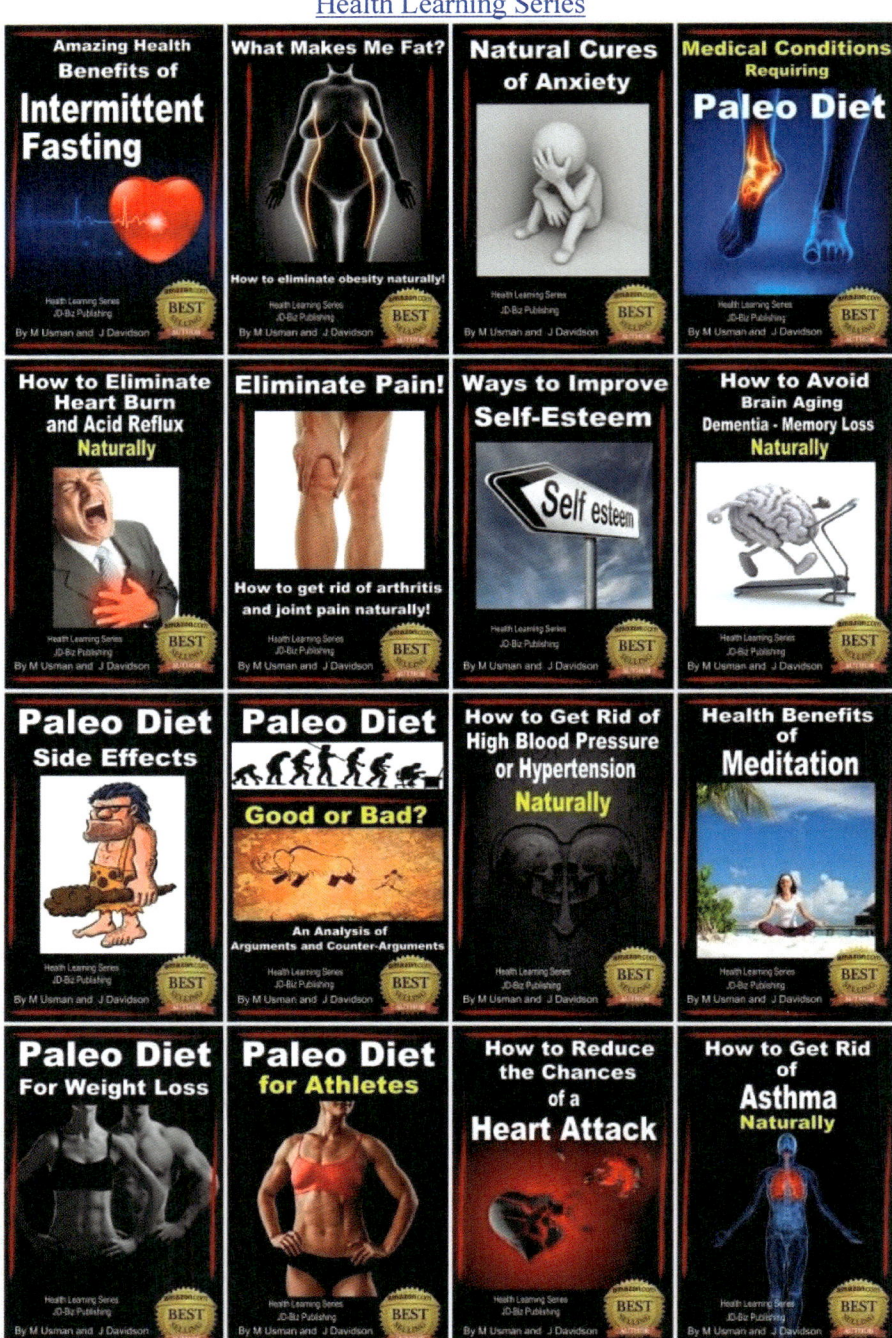

How to Raise Budgerigars

Amazing Animal Book Series

Learn To Draw Series

How to Build and Plan Books

How to Raise Budgerigars

Entrepreneur Book Series

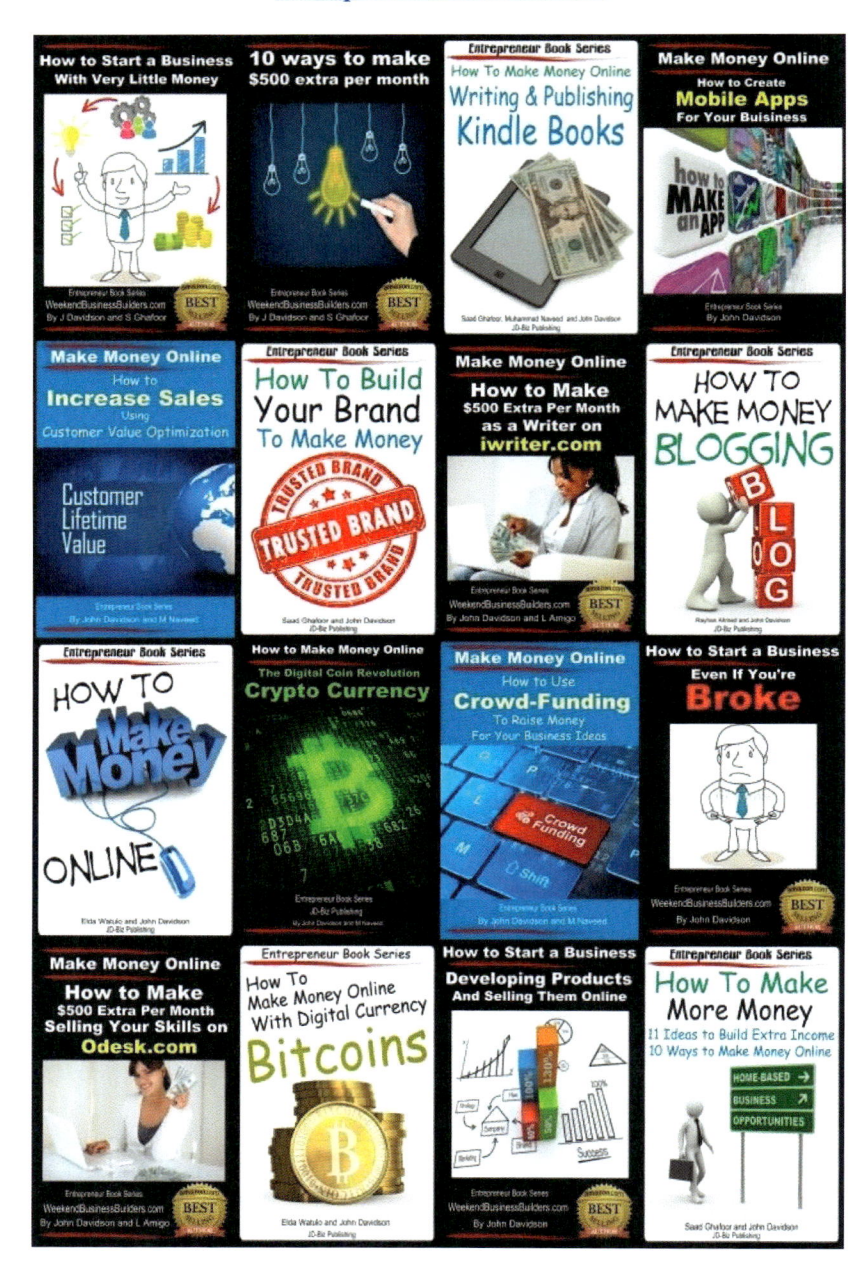

Our books are available at

1. Amazon.com
2. Barnes and Noble
3. Itunes
4. Kobo
5. Smashwords
6. Google Play Books

Download Free Books!

http://MendonCottageBooks.com

Publisher

JD-Biz Corp
P O Box 374
Mendon, Utah 84325
http://www.jd-biz.com/

Printed in Great Britain
by Amazon